D1244200

Starting a Business: Creating a Plan

Young Adult Library of Small Business and Finance

Building a Business in the Virtual World

Business & Ethics

Business & the Government: Law and Taxes

Business Funding & Finances

Keeping Your Business Organized:
Time Management & Workflow

Managing Employees

Marketing Your Business

Starting a Business: Creating a Plan

Understanding Business Math & Budgets

What Does It Mean to Be an Entrepreneur?

Young Adult Library of Small Business and Finance

Starting a Business: Creating a Plan

James Fischer

Mason Crest

Mason Crest
450 Parkway Drive, Suite D
Broomall, PA 19008
www.masoncrest.com

Printed in the United States of America.

First printing
9 8 7 6 5 4 3 2 1

Series ISBN: 978-1-4222-2912-5
Hardcover ISBN: 978-1-4222-2920-0
Paperback ISBN: 978-1-4222-2984-2
ebook ISBN: 978-1-4222-8910-5

The Library of Congress has cataloged the
hardcopy format(s) as follows:

Library of Congress Cataloging-in-Publication Data

Fischer, James, 1988-
  Starting a business : creating a plan / James Fischer.
    pages cm. — (Young adult library of small business and finance)
  Audience: Age 12
  Audience: Grade 7 to 8.
    ISBN 978-1-4222-2920-0 (hardcover) — ISBN 978-1-4222-2912-5 (series) — ISBN 978-1-4222-8910-5 (ebook) — ISBN 978-1-4222-2984-2 (pbk.)
  1. Business planning—Juvenile literature. 2. New business enterprises—Planning—Juvenile literature. 3. Small business—Planning—Juvenile literature. I. Title.
  HD30.28.F572 2014
  658.1'1—dc23
                                                2013016931

Produced by Vestal Creative Services.
www.vestalcreative.com

CONTENTS

INTRODUCTION

Brigitte Madrian, PhD

S mall businesses serve a dual role in our economy. They are the bedrock of community life in the United States, providing goods and services that we rely on day in and day out. Restaurants, dry cleaners, car repair shops, plumbers, painters, landscapers, hair salons, dance studios, and veterinary clinics are only a few of the many different types of local small business that are part of our daily lives. Small businesses are also important contributors to the engines of economic growth and innovation. Many of the successful companies that we admire today started as small businesses run out of bedrooms and garages, including Microsoft, Apple, Dell, and Facebook, to name only a few. Moreover, the founders of these companies were all very young when they started their firms. Great business ideas can come from people of any age. If you have a great idea, perhaps you would like to start your own small business. If so, you may be wondering: What does it take to start a business? And how can I make my business succeed?

A successful small business rests first and foremost on a great idea—a product or service that other people or businesses want and are willing to pay for. But a good idea is not enough. Successful businesses start with a plan. A business plan defines what the business will do, who its customers will be, where the firm will be located, how the firm will market the company's product, who the firm will hire, how the business will be financed, and what, if any, are the firm's plans for future growth. If a firm needs a loan from a bank in order to start up, the bank will mostly likely want to see a written business plan. Writing a business plan helps an entrepreneur think

Introduction

through all the possible road blocks that could keep a business from succeeding and can help convince a bank to make a loan to the firm.

Once a firm has the funding in place to open shop, the next challenge is to connect with the firm's potential customers. How will potential customers know that the company exists? And how will the firm convince these customers to purchase the company's product? In addition to finding customers, most successful businesses, even small ones, must also find employees. What types of employees should a firm hire? And how much should they be paid? How do you motivate employees to do their jobs well? And what do you do if employees don't get along? Managing employees is an important skill in running almost any successful small business.

Finally, firms must also understand the rules and regulations that govern how they operate their business. Some rules, like paying taxes, apply to all businesses. Other rules apply to only certain types of firms. Does the firm need a license to operate? Are there restrictions on where the firm can locate or when it can be open? What other regulations must the firm comply with?

Starting up a small business is a lot of work. But despite the hard work, most small business owners find their jobs

Starting a Business: Creating a Plan

rewarding. While many small business owners are happy to have their business stay small, some go on to grow their firms into more than they ever imagined, big companies that service customers throughout the world.

What will your small business do?

Brigitte Madrian, PhD
Aetna Professor of Public Policy and Corporate Management
Harvard Kennedy School

ONE

Why Do You Need a Business Plan?

Y ou're walking to your friend's house, but you've never been to his house before. You think you know how to find the street he lives on, but you've never really walked to that neighborhood.

At first, everything seems pretty familiar as you walk through your own neighborhood. Then things start to look strange and unfamiliar. You didn't bring a map with you, so you can't figure out where you are, or how to get to your friend's house. You should have brought that map!

GRANT APPLICATION

Your full name (**exactly as it appears on your Social Security card**)

1. Last name

4. Number and street (include apt. number)

5. City (and country if not U.S.)

8. Your Social Security Number

Thorough business plans can give grant makers or banks confidence that you will use their money wisely.

Starting a Business: Creating a Plan

Running a business without a business plan is a little like not bringing a map when you're going somewhere unfamiliar. Business plans are basically maps for businesses.

Without a business map—a plan—you could get lost very easily. Business plans map out what your business goals are, and how you are going to achieve them. You'll find it a lot easier to find your way with a business plan!

Reasons for a Plan

For businesses just starting out, business plans are mostly for the person starting the business. If you are about to start your own business, a business plan will be very helpful. Plans organize your thoughts and help you decide where you're going and how you'll get there.

But business plans have a few other purposes too. Business plans can help you raise money to improve and grow your business. Maybe you know someone who wants to *invest* in your business, but she's not sure you'll be responsible enough to use the money right. If you can hand her a business plan, she'll know you are very responsible and serious about your business. She can also see exactly how you will use the money and what you want your business to achieve. You're much more likely to get the money.

In general, people will take your business a lot more seriously when they see you have a business plan. As a young person running a business, not everyone may take you seriously because of your age. You have to prove them wrong. They'll change their mind once they see all the time and effort you've put into creating a plan.

You might also use your plan to convince people to do business with you. For example, you might need to buy a lot of fabric to sell clothes. You want good, affordable fabric, and you find a company that could sell you a lot. If you can show the fabric company your business plan, the people at the company are more likely to give you good deals and treat you with respect.

Choosing When

Not all businesses start out with a business plan right away. Some people start a very small business, just selling their products or services a little at a time. Then their sales end up being successful, and all of a sudden, they have a real business!

Other people know they want to start a business. They just have to figure out how exactly to do it. They start out by wanting to run a business, even if they don't know what they are going to sell.

Both of these types of people should write a business plan. They might write one at different points in their business, though. The first person might decide to write a business plan when he needs to borrow some money to grow his business even more. At first, he wasn't really planning on running an organized business. But now that he is, he will need to write a business plan.

The second person will want to write a business plan right away, before she even starts the business. She'll have a much better idea of where the business is going and how she can achieve her goals with a business plan. She could start the business without a plan, but she won't be organized and the business will have a good chance of failing.

14

Plan Parts

Every business plan looks a little different. Business plans for really big companies might be hundreds of pages long and have a lot of complicated information. For small-business owners, business plans may be shorter, but no less important. Good business plans tend to have some of the same parts. They should give all the information you need to run a good business and reach your business goals.

The first part of a business plan is the **executive** summary. This part outlines and sums up what the rest of the plan says. Someone who doesn't have time to read the whole plan will read the executive summary. Many business plan writers have discovered that they write the executive summary last, once they know what is in the rest of their business plan. Think of it as being a little like the introduction to a school essay.

Another part should describe your company. What does your business do? And why does it exist? You can write about the history of your business and the goals you started out with. Include basic information about where you run your business, what you sell, and how your company is unique. Imagine the person reading this section knows absolutely nothing about your business. But when she reads it, she will have a very clear picture of your business.

The next section is a marketing plan. Marketing is how you connect your business to your customers. Your market is whom you sell to, including where you sell and to whom. Explain in more detail who your customers are and what your business will mean to them. Advertising goals and **strategies** go in this section. Answer the question, "Why would someone want to buy from me instead of a company that sells something similar?" Then include

A marketing plan encourages you to think ahead about what group of people make up your potential customers, how best to reach these people with your product or service, and why they should do business with you rather than a competitor.

information about how you will sell your service (something you'll do for your customers) or product (something you will make for your customers).

Along with the marketing plan, write a part about your competition. You are probably not the only business around selling whatever you're selling. Figure out who is selling similar things (those are your competitors), and write about what they are doing. This section helps you plan how you will stand out and stay ahead of your competition.

A section on organization and *management* should come next. You'll write about how you will run your company and if you have or will hire employees. You have to run your business from day to day—how will you do It? Include information like how many hours you will work a week and how you will manage employees.

Next, include a part on what you are selling. You could be selling a product, a physical thing like food or a toy. Or you could be selling a service, like mowing lawns or babysitting. No matter what you're selling, you should describe it and how you will make or *develop* it. Talk about how it benefits your customers. Basically, tell the story of your product or service.

Finally, include a section about finances, which means how you manage your business's money. Figure out how much money you will need to do everything you want to do. Also include a guess at how much money your business will make. The financial section is where a lot of numbers come in.

Business Plan Tips

You want your business plan to look *professional*, not sloppy. You're a serious businessperson so your business plan should be well put together.

A clear and concise layout for your business plan is your best bet. Big ideas speak for themselves.

Your plan should be simply and clearly worded. Don't use big words to impress people. They'll be impressed with the ideas, not the words. Use short sentences too, so people don't get lost reading your plan. You are writing a business plan, not a novel.

Use some charts in your plan. Excel charts, bar graphs, and pie charts can all make your information easier to see and understand. Make your charts simple, with easy-to-read numbers and labels. Charts and graphs can easily become confusing, but keep-

Starting a Business: Creating a Plan

ing them simple will really make your business plan look more professional. You can include them within each section, or make an appendix at the back with all the charts and additional information.

Stick to one font for your business plan, like Times New Roman. Don't try to use lots of crazy fonts to make your plan exciting. The exciting part is the ideas in your plan!

As for the format of the document itself, try not to cram all your writing together. Use page breaks to separate sections and to separate charts from the rest of the text. People will enjoy reading it more if it doesn't look too cramped and busy.

Finally, spell-check! Writing a business plan with lots of grammatical and spelling errors won't Impress anyone. Have someone edit your plan too, before you decide it's finished. Then people reading it will focus on your ideas and not get distracted by spelling mistakes.

LENGTH

You might be tempted to write lots and lots of pages in your business plan. Keeping it shorter is a better idea. You may have tons to say about your business, but people won't want to read a long, complicated plan. You might not even want to read it when you refer back to it later! Your plan shouldn't be much longer than thirty pages. Consider trimming your plan down if you find it getting too long. Use short sentences, and make sure everything you say is needed. Take out anything that doesn't absolutely need to be there.

Why Do You Need a Business Plan?

Printing your business plan professionally is a sign, both to yourself and potential investors, that your business is serious about success.

Starting a Business: Creating a Plan

Once you're happy with the writing and the charts, print out your plan and stick it in a binder or a report folder. You might even want to get it printed professionally, if you don't have a good printer for your business. You can get it printed on nice paper with no ink splotches or faded charts. Then keep your plan in a place you won't forget. You'll need to look at it again in the future, after you've used your plan to run your business.

Hello
my name is

???

TWO

What Will You Name Your Business? What Will Your Business Offer?

Two of the very first things you need to do when starting a business are figure out what you will sell and come up with a name. You obviously need something to sell if you're running a business. That's the point of businesses, after all. And imagine a business without a name—you'd never remember what the business did or how to find it!

In addition, you need to figure out what makes your business great and unique. Why should customers buy from you and not other businesses around town or online? If you don't answer this question, your business might not do so well.

In your business plan, you'll need to outline your products or services, your name, and how you will stand out from the crowd.

Take some time to really think about these things, and you'll be seeing your business grow in no time!

Selling

First thing's first: You'll have to choose exactly what you're selling with your business. Maybe you already have an idea or a hobby you want to turn into a business so you can make money. Or you like the idea of starting a business, but you aren't sure exactly what you want to sell.

Many young people, and older businesspeople as well, start businesses because they invent something that will help people solve a problem. Or they have a special skill or hobby they like to do, and they get so good at it they can do it for other people and get paid for it.

Young people turn ideas into businesses all the time. Just start with something you enjoy doing. Make a list of all the skills and hobbies you have. Pay attention to little problems you have or that you see other people struggling with. You could come up with a great idea to solve those problems.

Maybe you enjoy taking videos and then editing them on the computer. Right now, you just film your friends for fun and post videos on YouTube. You're getting pretty good at filming and editing, and you want to do something else with your skills. You also want to start making money, but you're not sure you really want to work for someone else. You'd rather be your own boss!

Then one day a friend of your parents' asks you to film her retirement party. She'll even give you some money. You go to the party, film it, edit the video, and give it back to her for $50. You just stumbled across a business idea! You decide you could turn your passion for making and editing videos into a business.

Starting a Business: Creating a Plan

QUESTIONS TO ASK WHEN NAMING

Ask yourself these questions while you're thinking of a good business name. The more yeses you answer, the better the name. (Adapted from How-to-Branding.com)

1. Is it easy to spell?
2. Is it easy to say?
3. Is it original?
4. Is it **universal**?
5. Does it convey what your company does?
6. Is it memorable?
7. Can you grow with this name, or will it become **obsolete**?

Naming

Now that you have a business idea, you need a name. Your business name is actually very important. Your name is the very first thing someone will know about your company. Good names communicate a lot about your business in a very simple way. You wouldn't want every **potential** customer asking you in confusion what your names means. You want them asking about what you're selling and why they should buy it.

You might think this is obvious, but you generally want your business's name to be a word or several words. A bunch of

What Will You Name Your Business?

Pick a name that hasn't been claimed by others. A quick web search and domain name search will alert you to any existing use.

 **Starting a Business: Creating a Plan**

numbers or letters strung together will not be memorable; people won't be likely to remember the name of your business.

Be creative with your names. You can even use words that don't exist, but don't just make up nonsense. The car name Acura is a good example. Acura isn't a real word. But it does make people think of the word "accuracy." People who want a car that works really well (just about everyone!) would be interested in a car whose name sounds like accuracy. The people who created the name wanted something unique and memorable, and also meaningful.

Take a look at all the products and advertisements around you. Pay attention to what makes good names good and bad names bad. Take a few days to think of names. Write down everything you think of, even if you think your ideas aren't that great. Eventually you'll come up with a few that are.

After you come up with a name, you'll need to do a little research. First, make sure no other business has the same name. If you copy a business's name, you are breaking the law and could get into trouble. You might want to think of a few good business names, so you can be sure you come up with one that hasn't already been taken by someone else.

Do a **trademark** search. Business names that are registered or trademarked with the U.S. government can't be copied. Go to the United States Patent and Trademark Office to do a search. Unfortunately, if you find another business with the name you want, you'll have to start thinking of other names. Even if it weren't illegal, you want your business to stand out anyway and not get confused with another business. Later on, you'll have to trademark your own business name so no one else can steal it.

Also check out your name on the Internet. You'll want to set up a website either now or someday soon. Lots of website addresses

What Will You Name Your Business? 27

A name that is easy to spell makes it simple for new customers to find you and existing customers to recommend you.

Starting a Business: Creating a Plan

have already been taken, so you should do a search of your business's name to see what comes up. If all the websites that look like the name of your business are taken, you might just want to create a new name.

You also should test out your name. Ask people you know what they think of your name choice. Find some people who are likely to become customers, and ask them what they think. They'll tell you whether they would consider buying from a business with that name, or if the name is too confusing or just sounds bad.

For your video business, you write down a long list of names, as you think about it over several days. You narrow it down to: Video Production Plus, Celebration Video, and Rewind.

You ask your friends what they think of the names, and then you do some Internet searching. Your friends liked Celebration Video the best. Video Production Plus sounded too formal and long, and Rewind was too vague. You do a trademark search, and find that Celebration Video is already trademarked. However, CelebrationVideos (without a space between the names, and with an extra "s") is not trademarked. You've found your business's name.

REGISTERING YOUR NAME

Once you pick your name, you'll have to register it. You usually have to register it with your state government. Check out your state's rules to figure out what you have to do because the rules are a little different state to state. In many places, you only have to register with your county, not the state. Call or visit your **county clerk** office or visit the office's website.

Your business's identity may be the only thing that sets you apart from your competition. A well-designed logo is an important part of building a strong identity for your business.

Starting a Business: Creating a Plan

Branding

You have your idea and your name, but you're still missing something before you can really start your business. That something is called branding. When you figure out how your business is different from similar businesses, you're working on branding.

You'll probably have to compete with lots of other businesses. But you'll also probably find there's plenty of room for your business, as long as you make it a little different.

You can brand your business in a few ways. Think of your brand as your image. Logos, colors, and even type can all add to your brand. For example, if you want your brand to be really serious, you could use a simple black and white logo and Times New Roman font on your business website, advertisements, brochures, and signs. If you want to sell to young people, you might use brighter colors and a fun font. Depending on how you brand yourself, different people will want to buy what you're selling.

For your video business, you want to have mostly adults hire you. You'll film at weddings, birthdays, and other parties. You want your brand to look professional and put together. You also want your brand to look lively and remind people of celebrations. Finally, you want people to think cutting-edge technology when they think of your business. Anyone can take a video at a wedding, but you have the skill, the camera, and the video-editing software to make a really nice video.

After a lot of thought and drawing on paper and on the computer, you come up with a good logo, a professional-looking website, and a design for an advertising flyer. Now you'll use the designs you created on everything you create that has to do with your business.

THREE

What Are Your Short-Term Objectives and Long-Term Goals?

Think back to the map example at the beginning of chapter 1. You were heading to a friend's house, but you didn't know how to get there. Then you got lost.

Your business plan, like the map, will get you where you're going. But you have to know where you're going in the first place. If you set out to find your friend's house but didn't even know what street it was on, you'd never get there, with or without a map. You would just wander around aimlessly.

The same thing is true in business. You have to have goals. Without goals, you won't necessarily even know where you're going. To run the best business possible, you'll need some goals. When you reach them, you'll know your business is successful.

Applying S.M.A.R.T. gives you a solid map for achieving any goal.

Starting a Business: Creating a Plan

S.M.A.R.T. Goals

Businesses often use an *acronym* called S.M.A.R.T. to talk about goals. S.M.A.R.T. goals lead to success!

S: Specific

Goals should be specific. Often, people will set really broad goals for themselves, like graduating from high school or becoming a star athlete. In business, people make broad goals like making a lot of money. You want your goals to be more specific than that, so you can figure out how to reach them. Instead of saying you want to make a lot of money, you could instead make it your goal to make $500 a month with your business in the first year.

M: Measureable

You won't really know you've reached a goal unless you can measure it. Numbers are best because you can keep track of them and then figure out when you've reached your goal. An immeasurable goal would be getting people to like your business. What does that mean, and how would you measure it? You can turn that into a measurable goal by saying you want 95 percent customer satisfaction. You can measure that by sending out surveys to customers asking them how their experience was buying from your business. When 95 percent of those surveys show that customers are happy, you'll have reached your goal.

A: Attainable

Attainable means able to be achieved. You'll find it frustrating if you set yourself goals you'll never be able to meet. Make sure your goals are something you really can work toward, and

Be realistic about how long it will take to reach a goal. You want these dates to keep you motivated, but you don't want them to stress you out!

Starting a Business: Creating a Plan

hopefully achieve. A very large business might be able to get 100,000 customers in one year, but if you're just starting out with a small business, you will probably not be able to reach that number of customers. When you end up with 900 customers after a year, you might think you've failed because you fell really short. But if you had set a much more realistic goal at 1,000 customers, you would be a lot closer to your goal!

R: RELEVANT

Your goals have to make sense. Choose goals that matter to you and your business. If your business is babysitting, you don't want to make a goal of selling fifty jars of homemade jam to your customers. You might want to sell jam, but that goal doesn't really have anything to do with your babysitting business. You should also make sure your goals are relevant to what you want to do with your business. Your goals should be exciting, and take your business in a direction you want it to go. Otherwise, you'll never try to work toward your goal because you won't actually want to.

T: TIME-BASED

Goals need a certain timeline. You could easily say that someday you want to hire an employee. To actually achieve that goal, you need to decide when you want an employee. Otherwise, it will be easy to push your goal further and further into the future. Decide when you want a new employee, like in the next year, or in the next six months. Then make a timeline and a plan for making that happen. Keep your goals' timelines to less than three years in the future.

You may plan to use social media like Facebook and Twitter to promote your business, but are you making sure that those kinds of tasks have measureable goals?

Starting a Business: Creating a Plan

Applying S.M.A.R.T. Goals to Your Business

How do all these pieces of advice apply to your video-production business? Let's take a look.

You're still just starting out, and you have only had one job so far. You have a ton of ideas and goals swarming around in your head, but you'll have to organize them and choose a few if you ever want to make any of them happen.

Your first goal is to get new customers. According to the S.M.A.R.T. goal *criteria*, you'll have to work on this goal a little bit before you can actually achieve it. Right now, it has a few problems.

Your goal isn't quite specific enough, and it doesn't have a timeline. You want new customers, but how many? And when? You decide you want ten new customers in the next three months. Now your goal is way more specific, and it even has a timeline. You can measure your goal—you either have ten new customers or you don't. Your goal is also relevant, and you think it's attainable.

Your second goal is to post flyers all over town in the next two months, advertising your business. This second goal already has a timeline, but you can make it a little more specific. You should decide how many flyers you want to post and where. Make a plan. Your advertising goal is relevant, and it is measurable because you can count how many flyers you hang up.

However, you have a lot to do at school over the next two weeks. Plus you're going to visit your grandparents this weekend. Maybe you don't really have time to hang up flyers all over town. Your goal isn't attainable. To make it more attainable, you can simply say you want to hang up flyers during the next month. You can hang them up when you can during the next two weeks. After that, you can spend more time hanging the rest and achieve your goal. You'll feel like you're accomplishing something, instead of getting frustrated about not getting anything done.

Long- and Short-Term Goals

Long-term goals are the ways in which you want your business to grow and change. You might not be working on them right now, but you will in the next few months or years.

You can think of long-term goals in different categories. You can set financial goals for how much money you want your business to make. You can set growth goals, which focus on how you want your business to expand, opening stores or hiring employees. Service goals have to do with keeping customers and making them happy. And social goals focus on making the world better by doing things like volunteering and donating some of your **profits**.

Goals you want to achieve right away are different from goals you want to achieve months or even years in the future. Goals you want to work toward right now are called objectives.

Short-term objectives are how you work toward your longer-term goals. You make a series of smaller goals that will be achieved soon. In a few years, when you add up all the objectives, you'll have achieved your bigger, long-term goal!

Both kinds of goals go hand-in-hand. Your long-term goal might be to open a storefront. If you're just starting out, opening a store probably isn't a very realistic goal, but it might be a good long-term goal. In the meantime, your short-term objectives could be working toward a store. You will need a lot of customers before opening a store is worthwhile. You will also need a lot of money.

Starting a Business: Creating a Plan

And a business *loan*. Each one of those can be made into a specific objective.

GOALS AND YOUR BUSINESS PLAN

Business plans don't always include a specific section on goals, though you can if you want to. Another choice you have is to just set some goals and objectives and then remember them throughout your plan. You're goals should shine through everything else you write in your plan. For example, if your goal is to help your surrounding community as much as possible, you will describe your business as community-oriented and focused on helping people. In your financial section, you might say you plan on donating 10 percent of your profits to local charities. In your business management section, you can decide you want to give any future employees a paid day off every month to volunteer at a charity.

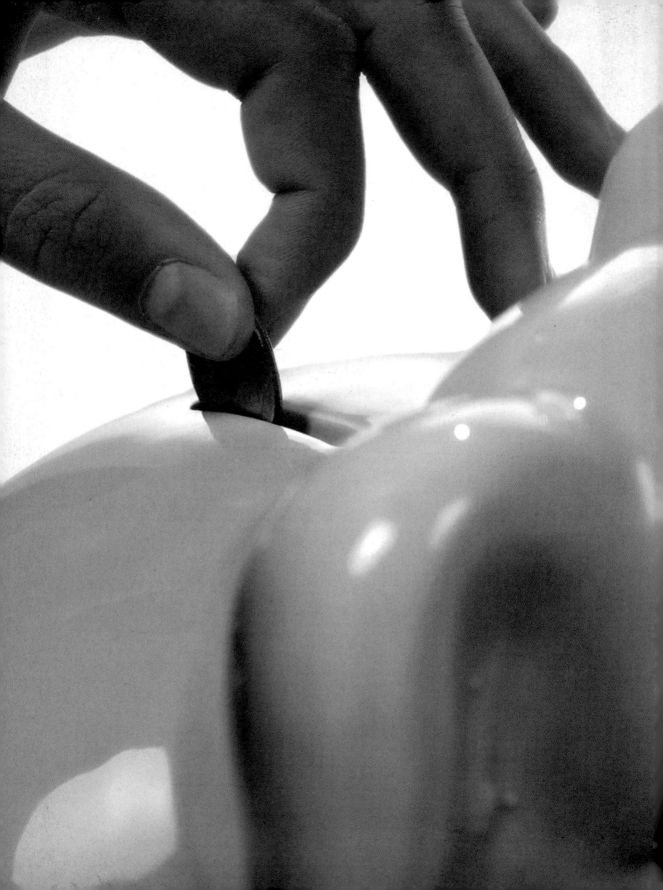

FOUR

Financing

Once you start a business, you'll quickly find it takes money to make money. You need money for everything from advertising to buying a **domain name** for a website to shipping a product you sell to people who bought it online.

Hopefully, you'll end up making more money than you're spending. Then you know you have a successful business!

Connecting Your Goals and Money

Every goal you have will probably take some money to achieve. Think about your goals, and see if you can *estimate* how much money you will need to make them happen.

In your business plan, pay attention to the financial section. You won't know exactly how much money you'll need, or how much you'll make, but you can guess. The financial part of a business plan is where you can connect your business goals and money. Do some research about how much other people have had to spend to start small businesses.

Make your financial section very specific. Don't worry that what actually happens may turn out to be different than your guesses. You just want to have an idea of where you are going, and how much money you will need as you grow your business.

For your video business, you break down your financial needs into parts. You'll need $20 to print and hang up flyers. You'll need $10 to buy a domain name for a website. You'll need $50 to legally register your business with your town. And you'll need $100 for a new piece of video editing software. Altogether, you'll need $180 to even start your business.

Later on, you'll need some more money for advertising. You think you might even need brand-new, top-of-the-line video editing software and a new computer a year from now. Then you might need $2,500.

Savings

The first place you should look for money to start a business is your savings. Many young people have a savings account, which has money they have saved up for a few years. Other young people might keep piggy banks, or have a little money stashed somewhere else.

Of course, your savings might be for a car, college, or something else very important. Before you spend any of your savings

on your business, decide how much you really care about your business. Talk to your family to see what they think.

If you don't have much savings now, don't worry! Start saving. Save your allowance. Save any money you get for your birthday or holidays. Save money you make doing small jobs like babysitting or walking dogs. Give yourself a few months to save money. In the meantime, you can be planning out your business and writing your business plan.

For your video business, say you have a little bit of savings, but not quite enough to cover the $180 you need right away. You work on your business plan, design your website, and save your money. After just a month, you have enough to add to your savings to cover all the costs.

Borrowing from Friends and Family

If you just can't save up enough, you might also borrow money from friends and family. Borrowing money can be tricky, though, because you have to make absolutely sure you pay people back.

Family is a good place to start. Your parents, grandparents, aunts, uncles, and other adult members of your family might want to help you. Some of your friends might also want to help you.

You have to prove you're going to be a responsible borrower, and that you have a good chance of making money. That's where your business plan comes in. You can show your business plan to people who might want to lend you money. They can read it over, decide they think your business is a good idea, and then lend you some money. Even just seeing you have a business plan might convince them. You must be responsible and hard working if you created a business plan!

When you borrow money from people you know, you need to pay them back, even if your business doesn't make any money. Have a plan for paying people back, no matter what. Start saving your spending money so you'll have at least a little to pay them back if your business isn't successful. Talk with your lenders and figure out how and when you will pay them back, no matter what.

Bank Loans

Instead of borrowing from your friends and family, you can take out a loan from banks. Loans are great for small businesses that need some money to really get going.

SMALL BUSINESS ASSOCIATION LOANS

A part of the government called the Small Business Administration (SBA) helps small businesses throughout the country. The SBA provides information and services for starting and growing small businesses. Part of that is funding small loans for businesses that need them. They are easier to get than some regular bank business loans, and give you a long time to pay them off. Like with other loans, you have to be at least eighteen or have a cosigner (one of your parents, for example). You'll apply for SBA loans through a bank, so ask at your bank if you're interested.

Starting a Business: Creating a Plan

You won't be able to take out very small loans. Banks won't lend you $100, for example. But they might lend you $5,000. Taking out loans is a good idea if you have some bigger **expenses** coming up, and don't have nearly enough savings to pay for them. When you need a new computer and video-editing software for your video business, you might consider taking out a loan.

Banks don't offer loans for free, though. You have to pay for them. When you take out a loan, banks will charge you interest, which is basically a **fee** you pay for borrowing the money.

You usually have a little time to start using the money you borrowed before you have to pay it back. Then you pay back a little bit each month. You have to pay back the original amount, plus the interest that the bank charges.

If you want a loan, you will have to apply for one at your bank. Only people over the age of eighteen can apply for loans. Business owners under age eighteen will have to have an adult officially be responsible for paying back the loan. In bank language, the adult will co-sign the loan.

After you fill out the application, you'll hear back from the bank about whether or not it will give you the loan. If you get the loan, you're free to spend the money to grow your business.

Investors

You have another possibility for financing your business—investors. People who agree to invest give a business money with the expectation they will get some money back in the future.

Investing is different from lending money. Investors only start to make their money back when the business they invested in starts to make money. They also hope to make a lot more money than they originally invested. Lenders get their money back from

the person they loaned to no matter what. Investors only invest when they are pretty sure they will make money on a business.

Again, a good business plan really helps you get money. People who might be interested in investing in your business will want to see a business plan. They want to see if you have good ideas, and if you are likely to make money. A good business plan, complete with good business ideas, will convince people to invest. Not having a business plan won't impress any investors, and they won't think you're taking your business seriously.

LOAN APPLICATIONS

Loan applications are different depending on the bank you're working with. However, most loan applications will ask you some similar things, like:

- your reasons for applying for a loan.
- how you will use the loan.
- what you need to buy specifically, and who will you buy it from.
- whether or not you have other loans and debts, and to whom you owe money.
- who will be managing the loan.
- personal information, including addresses, criminal record, and education.

Investors might be people in your town or city who want to see new small businesses grow. You might find an investor who really wants to help young *entrepreneurs* in particular. You can find investors by doing research online and by asking other business owners if they know of anyone to contact. An investor might even contact you because she heard about your business and wants to help out!

Grants

Yet another way to raise money for your business is to get grants. Grants are basically like gifts of money given to businesses and other organizations.

Lots of places give out grants to small businesses. The national government, state governments, and local governments have many grants for small businesses. So do some *trade groups* and bigger companies. You'll be able to find plenty of grants online if you do some research.

As with loans, you need to apply for grants. Unlike loans, though, a lot of people are competing for them. An organization might only give out one grant, but a hundred or more businesses apply for it.

Some grants require you to send in a business plan. A really good business plan might convince the grant givers to pick you! And a really bad one or a nonexistent one might get you thrown out of consideration for the grant.

Don't get discouraged if you apply for several grants and don't get any. Just keep trying—every time you write a grant application, you get better and better at it.

Real-Life Financing

The TiE Young Entrepreneurs Business Plan Competition takes place every year. Thousands of students all over the world compete to win money to start businesses. Whether or not they win is based on how good their business plans are.

In the Ohio branch of the competition, many young high-school entrepreneurs competed to see who had the best business plan to start a business for less than $1,000. The winner was Anamika Veeramani, a junior from an Ohio high school. She won with a business plan for an online science journal for high school students.

CROWDFUNDING

The Internet has opened up lots of possibilities for funding businesses. One way you can raise money to start or grow your business is through crowdfunding websites. The idea behind crowdfunding sites is to get a little bit of money from a lot of people. Asking hundreds or even thousands of people to help you start a business isn't so hard on the Internet. Websites like Kickstarter or Indiegogo make it easy. Just sign up for an account on a crowdfunding website. You'll need to set up a page for your business, where you explain why you're asking for money, and what your financial goals are. The more convincing you are, the more money you'll get. Once you start up your page, you can send e-mails to people you know, who can then tell other people they know, and so on. You'll probably get people you've never even met giving you money!

Starting a Business: Creating a Plan

Anamika not only won the competition, but she won the funding for her business, all because of her business plan! She doesn't let her age stop her from doing what she wants to do. The science journal she created is run by high schoolers, and it publishes research done by high schoolers. She says, "I would do really well at science fairs, but there was nothing beyond that and no opportunities to publish in journals." She explains she started the journal, "because I wanted to stress the fact that while age and experience are closely tied, age and knowledge or ability don't necessarily **correlate**." Young people can do anything, even create businesses!

With a combination of a good business proposal, well-thought-out finances, and some hard work, you can get enough money to help your business grow. Learn how to raise and spend your money wisely, and you'll make it back with more customers and more profits.

Plan A

Plan B

Plan C

FIVE

Revising Your Plan

You've created a business plan, started your company, and business is booming! Now what? Now you'll need to revisit your business plan.

A business plan isn't something you create and then never look at again. You should look at it again and again to see if you're on track with your plan. And you can change your plan if it doesn't make sense for your business anymore.

Look It Over

Figure out a regular time to review your business plan. When you're first starting out, you might even want to review it every month. You can make time at the end of every month to check your plan, make sure you're following it, and see if you need to change anything.

Reading your business plan has a couple goals. First, you want to see that the decisions you've made about your business actually follow your business plan. Remember, you made the plan as a guide. Use it!

Second, you should read over the plan to see if you need to change anything. Every business plan needs to be changed from time to time, especially when a business is first starting. Keep on the lookout for spots in your plan that don't make sense anymore.

You might find yourself just reading it, and saying, "Okay, looks good." You need to really read it in-depth, though, and ask yourself some questions. Are you working toward achieving your goals? Are you on schedule? Does your financial section make sense now that you've started really doing business? If you're worried about your answers to any of those questions, you may need to change your plan.

You should also take a look at your plan when things are starting to go wrong. If you suddenly notice you're not making as much money as you used to, or if another competitor opens up a business near you, don't panic. Just look at your business plan, and see if you can come up with any solutions.

Change It

Your business plan is not carved in stone. You can change it whenever you want, but you should change it wisely.

Avoid taking out your plan and changing it all at once, just because you're bored. Whatever your business plan says is what your business does. Only make changes that are really necessary and will make your business better.

THE ONE-PAGE BUSINESS PLAN

The Young Entrepreneur website offers a solution for young people who don't have the time to write out a long business plan, or who just don't see the point—a one-page business plan. Here is the outline:

Vision: Explain what your business is and what you want to do with it.

Mission: Your mission is why you want to start your business in the first place. Discuss the end result of your work and how you will accomplish your vision.

Objectives: Make a bullet-point list of your short-term business goals. You don't have to be really detailed, just list the end goals.

Strategies: Talk about how you will achieve your objectives. This can be a bulleted list too.

Action Plans: Write down when you will achieve your objectives and how much money it will take. Be most specific in this section.

When something is going wrong, first review your business plan. Then you change it if you need to.

For example, maybe you're behind on an advertising project for your video production business. You're trying to put advertisements on local organization's websites. In return, you agree to put up ads for those organizations on your own website.

You want to get the whole thing done in a month, but you're two weeks in, and you haven't done much. You take a look at your business plan to figure out if you're just being lazy, or if there is a problem with your business.

Revising Your Plan 55

CHANGE YOUR PLAN WHEN...

Here are a few examples of when you should take another look at your business plan, and make some changes:

- A new competitor opens.
- Several of your customers complain about customer service.
- You realize you're not making as much money as you used to.
- Your employees are unhappy.
- New technologies appear that could make your business better (or compete with it).
- You grow a lot, and your original business model doesn't make sense anymore.

As you read your plan over, you notice that you've never mentioned hiring any employees. You're supposed to do all the work, including the filming, the editing, the advertising, the **bookkeeping**, and more. You just don't have time for everything! Maybe hiring an employee part time would be a good idea, you think.

Next you look at the financial section. You've added all your financial reports to your plan, so you have all the information you need right there. You see that you've actually made more money than you had estimated you'd make by now, so you have a little extra to spend. You do some more calculations and see that you could afford to hire someone to do advertising for you three hours a week. Your business plan made your problem a lot easier to see and solve.

Building a business might just be a daydream for you right now, or you might be right in the middle of running a business. Either way, business plans will be helpful. You can plan your business, practice business skills, and convince people to give your business money. The first step is to start writing! Join the millions of other people, including young business owners, who have written their own business plans and found success.

Revising Your Plan

Find Out More

ONLINE

Creating Smart Goals
topachievement.com/smart.html

Entrepreneur
www.entrepreneur.com

Teaching Kids Business
www.teachingkidsbusiness.com/business-basics-intro.htm

TYE Global Program (TiE Young Entrepreneurs)
www.tie.org/tyeglobal

U.S. Small Business Plan: Create Your Business Plan
www.sba.gov/category/navigation-structure/starting-managing-
business/starting-business/how-write-business-plan

IN BOOKS

Bachel, Beverly. *What Do You Really Want? How to Set a Goal and Go for It!* Minneapolis, Minn.: Free Spirit Publishing, 2001.

Bernstein, Daryl. *Better Than a Lemonade Stand! Small Business Ideas for Kids*. New York: Aladdin, 2012.

Daniels, Kathryn. *Common Sense Business for Kids*. Placerville, Calif.: Bluestocking Press, 2006.

Segel, Rick. *Retail Business Kit For Dummies*. Hoboken, N.J.: Wiley Publishing, 2008.

Vocabulary

Acronym: a word formed from the first letters of other words.

Bookkeeping: recording the money made and spent by a business.

County clerk: a government official at the county level who is in charge of elections and other government business.

Correlate: connected, happening at the same time.

Criteria: a standard used for judging.

Develop: to become or grow.

Domain name: a website address.

Entrepreneurs: business owners who take risks in order to get their business started.

Estimate: guess.

Executive: having to do with the power to make decisions in a business.

Expenses: money spent on something.

Fee: money charged for the use of a service.

Invest: to spend or give money with the expectation of making more money as a consequence in the future.

Loan: Money that you borrow and have to pay back later.

Management: responsibility for the organization of a business.

Obsolete: out of date; no longer used or produced.

Potential: having the ability to become something.

Professional: competent and skilled in a way that's appropriate for a job for which you are paid.

Professional: Having to do with something you do for a living.

Profits: the money a business makes after it accounts for all its expenses.

Strategies: specific plans for reaching a goal.
Trade groups: organizations specific types of businesses use to communicate with each other.
Trademark: a word or symbol legally established as belonging to an organization.
Universal: applicable and understandable to everyone

Index

61

About the Author and Consultant

James Fischer received his master's in education from the State University of New York, and went on to teach life skills to middle school students with learning disabilities.

Brigitte Madrian is the Aetna Professor of Public Policy and Corporate Management at the Harvard Kennedy School. Before coming to Harvard in 2006, she was on the faculty at the University of Pennsylvania Wharton School (2003–2006), the University of Chicago Graduate School of Business (1995–2003) and the Harvard University Economics Department (1993–1995). She is also a research associate and co-director of the Household Finance working group at the National Bureau of Economic Research. Dr. Madrian received her PhD in economics from the Massachusetts Institute of Technology and studied economics as an undergraduate at Brigham Young University. She is the recipient of the National Academy of Social Insurance Dissertation Prize (first place, 1994) and a two-time recipient of the TIAA-CREF Paul A. Samuelson Award for Scholarly Research on Lifelong Financial Security (2002 and 2011).

Picture Credits